Charles Santore
Snow White
COLORING BOOK

Award-winning artist Charles Santore has illustrated more than twenty children's picture books, including *Aesop's Fables*, *The Wizard of Oz*, and *The Velveteen Rabbit*. In addition to these touchstones of children's literature, Santore has written and illustrated storybooks of his own, including *The Silk Princess* and *A Stowaway on Noah's Ark*.

     Santore began his career as a commercial illustrator, working for advertising agencies and magazines. In the 1980s he turned to children's illustration, beginning with *The Tales of Peter Rabbit*. Each book can take up to two years to complete, which gives him time to develop the characters and the worlds they live in. Inside this coloring book are twenty-one black-and-white drawings that Santore made in preparation for his watercolor illustrations for *Snow White*. The lush, full-color illustrations are reproduced on the inside of the front and back covers. We've also included two blank pages at the end of the book, so you can draw and color your favorite characters from *Snow White*, or perhaps make up a fairy tale of your own.

Pomegranate

All artworks by Charles Santore (American). Black-and-white preparatory drawings are for watercolor illustrations from *Snow White* (Sterling Publishing, 2010).

1. Snow White's mother dreams of having a child.
2. Snow White's stepmother, the evil queen, asks her mirror, "Who is fairest of us all?"
3. One day the mirror answers the queen, "Snow White is fairer far than you."
4. The queen orders a huntsman to take Snow White into the woods and kill her.
5. Snow White begs the huntsman to spare her life.
6. The huntsman frees Snow White, and she runs through the woods.
7. Snow White finds a cottage with seven little chairs and seven little beds.
8. Snow White falls asleep in the cottage.
9. The seven dwarfs return home.
10. In the morning, Snow White tells the dwarfs what happened.
11. The dwarfs head out to dig for gold, and Snow White stays home alone.
12. The queen tricks Snow White into letting her into the cottage by showing her lace.
13. The queen tricks Snow White again by offering to comb her hair.
14. The queen prepares a poison apple to kill Snow White once and for all.
15. The queen fools Snow White by putting poison in only half of the apple.
16. Snow White takes a bite of the poisoned apple and dies.
17. The dwarfs mourn Snow White for three days.
18. The dwarfs carry Snow White's glass coffin to the top of the mountain.
19. A prince asks the dwarfs if he may take Snow White back to his palace.
20. Snow White awakens.
21. The prince and Snow White get married.

....

Pomegranate Communications, Inc.
19018 NE Portal Way, Portland OR 97230
800 227 1428   www.pomegranate.com

© 2016 Charles Santore
Item No. CB178
Designed by Tristen Jackman
Printed in Korea

25 24 23 22 21 20 19 18 17 16   10 9 8 7 6 5 4 3 2 1

Distributed by Pomegranate Europe Ltd.
Unit 1, Heathcote Business Centre, Hurlbutt Road
Warwick, Warwickshire CV34 6TD, UK
[+44] 0 1926 430111
sales@pomeurope.co.uk

This product is in compliance with the Consumer Product Safety Improvement Act of 2008 (CPSIA) and any subsequent amendments thereto. A General Conformity Certificate concerning Pomegranate's compliance with the CPSIA is available on our website at www.pomegranate.com, or by request at 800 227 1428. For additional CPSIA-required tracking details, contact Pomegranate at 800 227 1428.

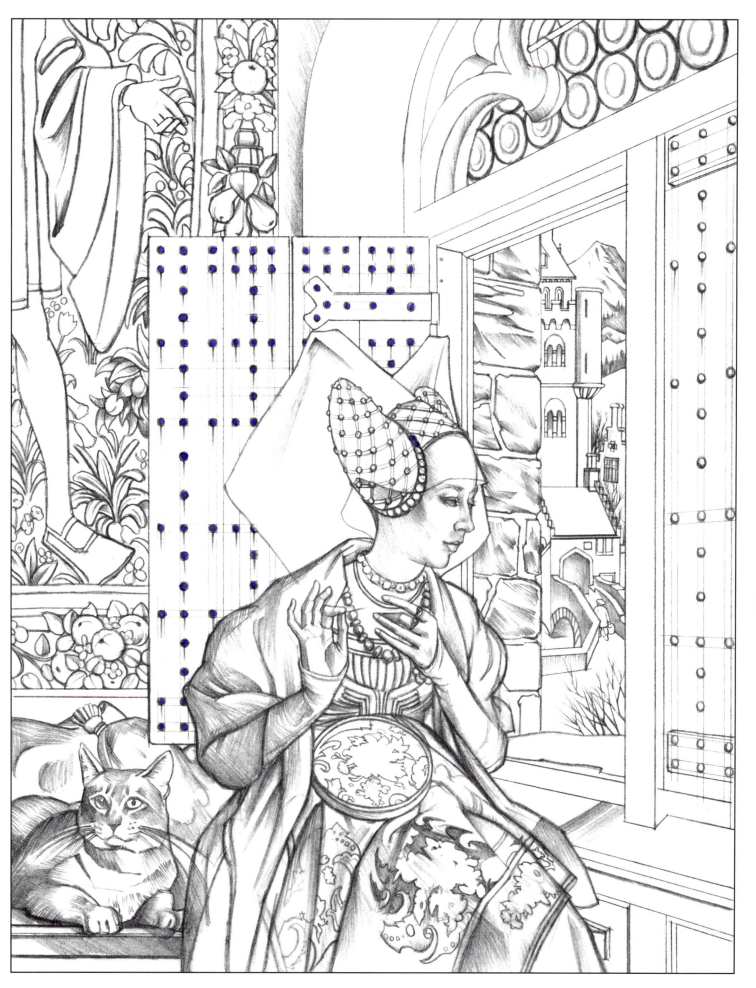

1. Snow White's mother dreams of having a child.

2. Snow White's stepmother, the evil queen, asks her mirror, "Who is fairest of us all?"

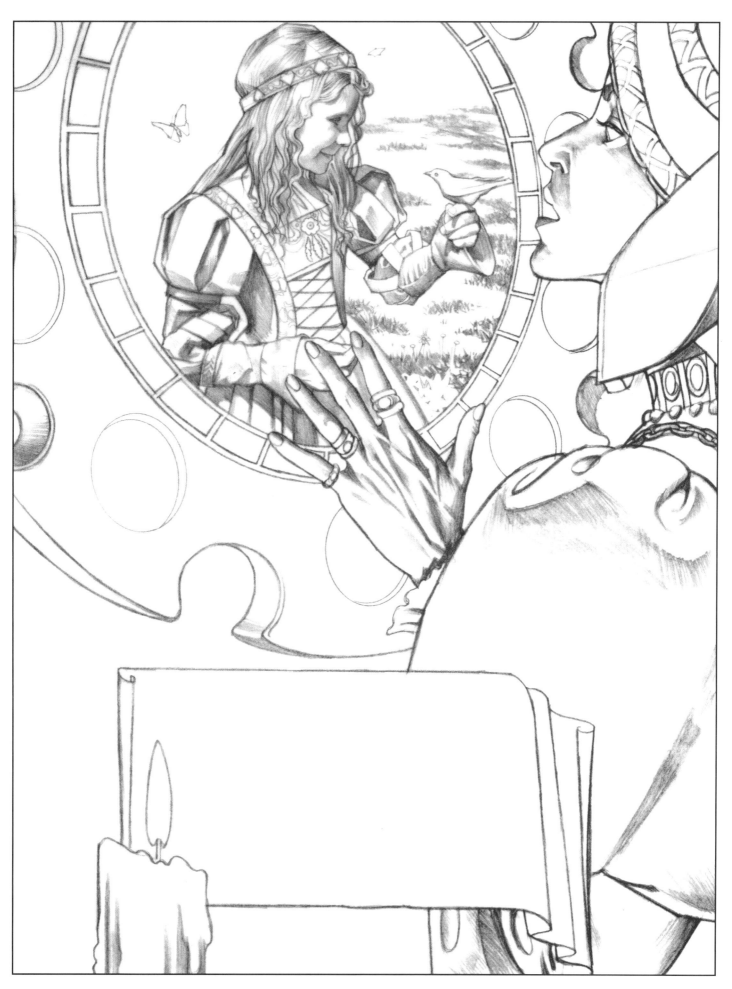

3. One day the mirror answers the queen, "Snow White is fairer far than you."

4. The queen orders a huntsman to take Snow White into the woods and kill her.

5. Snow White begs the huntsman to spare her life.

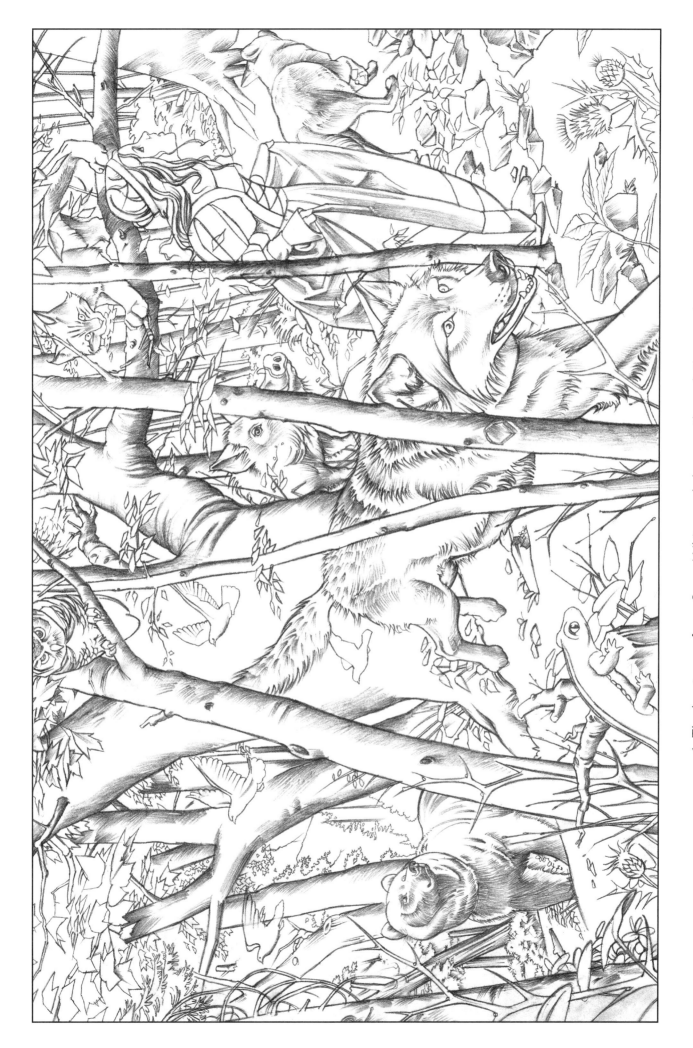

6. The huntsman frees Snow White, and she runs through the woods.

7. Snow White finds a cottage with seven little chairs and seven little beds.

8. Snow White falls asleep in the cottage.

9. The seven dwarfs return home.

10. In the morning, Snow White tells the dwarfs what happened.

11. The dwarfs head out to dig for gold, and Snow White stays home alone.

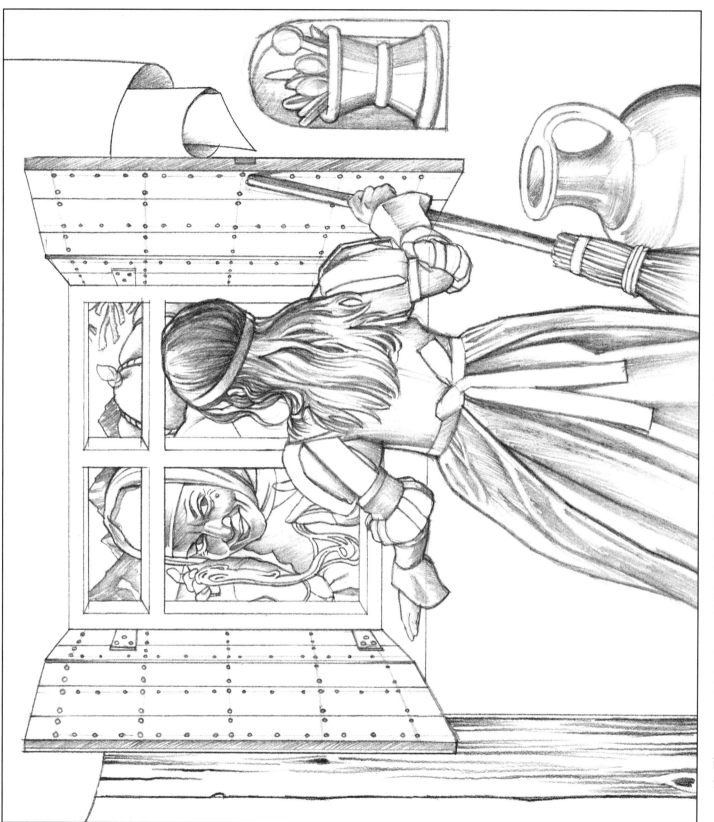

12. The queen tricks Snow White into letting her in and steals Snow White's breath by lacing her dress too tightly.

13. The queen tricks Snow White again by offering to comb her hair—with a poisonous comb.

14. The queen prepares a poisoned apple to kill Snow White once and for all.

15. The queen fools Snow White by having put poison in only half of the apple.

16. Snow White takes a bite of the poisoned apple and dies.

17. The dwarfs mourn Snow White for three days.

18. The dwarfs carry Snow White's glass coffin to the top of the mountain.

19. A prince asks the dwarfs if he may take Snow White back to his palace.

20. Snow White awakens.

21. The prince and Snow White get married.

Draw and color your own picture here!

Draw and color your own picture here!